MW01104922

KITTY HAIKU

(Haiku for Cat Lovers)

J. L. Williams

HARA
PUBLISHING GROUP

Published by
Hara Publishing
P.O. Box 19732
Seattle, WA 98109

ISBN: 1-887542-01-9

Library of Congress Catalog Card Number:
2003105946

Manufactured in Canada
10 9 8 7 6 5 4 3 2

Cover Design: Scott Fisher
Production: Scott and Shirley Fisher

*To cat lovers all over the world, without whom
the dog lovers of the world would simply take over.*

FOREWARNED

From the far distant reaches of childish memory, I cast back to find the first haiku I can ever remember. Impossible to tell from whence it came or by whom written. Suffice it to say I remember only the general gist of the thing, and have only recently hammered it back into the haiku *discipline*. It goes something like this, with due apologies to anyone ever associated with it:

> Full moon climbs the sky.
> Fetch a stick to hold it by.
> Lo! --a pretty fan!

Why should this haiku, this tag end of Japanese literature, stay so firmly ensconced in my memory? I haven't the faintest idea. I'm glad it did though, for now, a whole lifetime later, here I am with my own literary haiku endeavor. Notice how it follows a very strict form: the first line is five syllables long; the second, seven syllables; the third, five syllables. Couple this unvarying rule with a bucolic theme, and you have the makings of a haiku. It's trickier than it first appears. As to the bucolic, or pastoral, theme of my work, I have found fit to limit it pretty much to cats.

This has given rise to a new genre of haiku for which I am happy to take credit: the *Williamsonian* Haiku. It follows its own rules governing *caesura*, internal rhyme schemes and terminal rhyme patterns, which is to say, those rules that *I* have seen fit to impose on it.

My special thanks and kudos go to the cats in my house and in the neighborhood. This means **Roger**, whose usually silent presence pervades, penetrates, and permeates the premises. He occupies a generous amount of space in this life. **Spirit** and **Shadow** move about in ways reminiscent of their names. They lurk in the recesses of the house and in the back of one's psyche. Then there's **Ms. Kitty Karlyle**, a veritable vision of feline pulchritude who hails from next door. Her owners insist that there is no resemblance between her name and anyone else's, living or dead. Then there's **Riley**, erstwhile consort and lover of Ms. Kitty, also from next door, but who is now only with us in fond memory, having unceremoniously bit the dust in a territorial dispute with a Weimaraner ("him" of the canine persuasion). Surely, we cannot forget **Mephistopheles** from down the street, and **Max Manx**, his side-kick.

Kudos, too, to all others figuring on these pages, but whose names have slipped me.

Happy haiku!

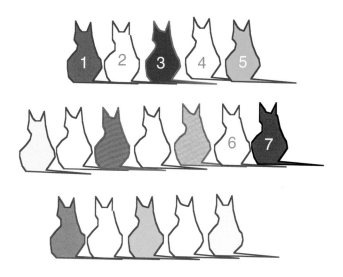

HAIKU

Write with *discipline:*
five syllables, then seven;
then another five.

KITTY HAIKU I

Use the discipline.
Then throw in a cat or two
just to stir things up.

KITTY HAIKU II

Write out the haiku
while maintaining cats in mind
Why? It *is* their due.

TOGETHER

Birds of a feather
flock together. So do cats:
Spirit and Shadow . . .

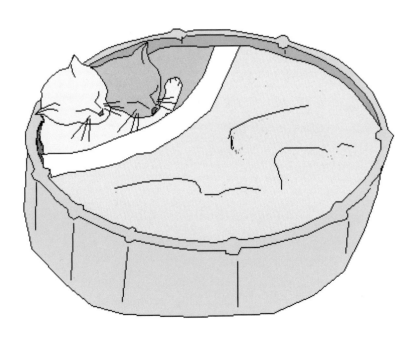

TEA

Now nothing remains
of the tea ceremony . . .
just the cat asleep.

PRIVATEER

Our Jolly Roger,
swashbuckling, boastful and brave,
rules the whole backyard.

NEMESIS

Roger's nemesis
lives down the street, his name is
Mephistopheles!

BEYOND NINE LIVES

There is just One Cat.
Through countless generations
he enjoys his life.

WISHFUL THINKING

Three little frogs hop
near the invisible cat;
three frogs, then two . . . hop!

IF...

In this perfect world
there are no imperfections
then why do frogs...croak?

MYSTIQUE

Uninhibited
gaze, mysterious ways. That's
Ms. Kitty Karlyle.

NIGHT VISITORS

Five little haiku
crept into my sleep last night--
one... two... three... four... five!

BIG IDEAS

Can big ideas
be squeezed into small haikus?
Ah, there's the challenge.

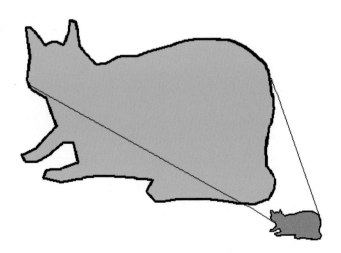

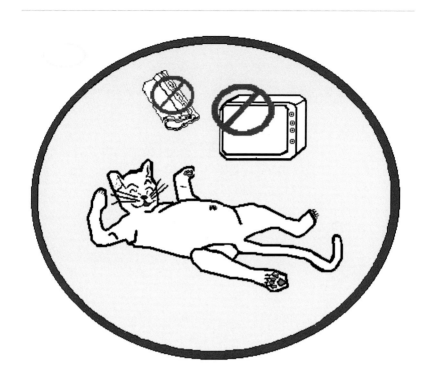

NEED

Cancel the papers.
Turn off the television.
Kittens need to play.

QUESTION ON WAKING UP

I threw Roger out
this morning at two-thirty.
How'd he get back in?

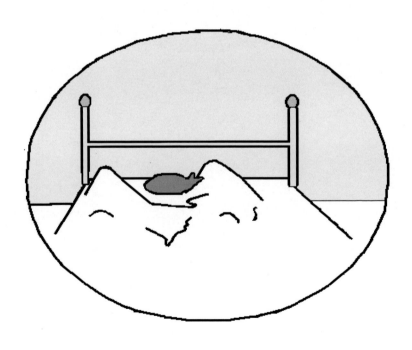

FASCINATION

Sea plane circles down
breaking through low lying clouds
to a smooth landing.

NURSERY RHYME

Great "A," little "a,"
Bouncing "B." Cat's in cupboard?
Mephistophilee!!

TAILLESS TALES

Room full of rockers
is a cat's idea of Hell--
tales Manx *love* to tell.

BUTTERFLIES

Cats and butterflies--
two widely spaced opposites.
How vast is God's mind!

ROGER

Roger likes to sleep
wherever it's nice and warm.
Dream mice --take cover!

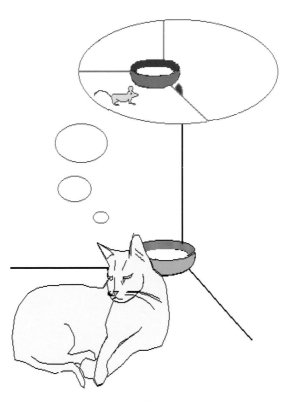

Egyptian Statue

Cat was first conceived
in the mind of God: shining,
pure contemplation.

Outlook

Centered and serene
he gazes out on turmoil
at peace with himself.

Secret

Cats know this secret:
Attitude is everything.
--wisdom of a king.

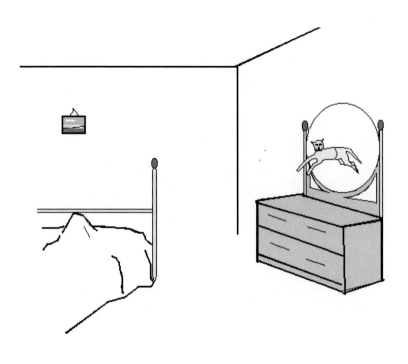

BOUNDING

Haiku comes bounding
from a special place where joy
boundlessly abounds.

SENTINELS TWO

Spirit and Shadow
keep the yard's perimeters:
self-appointed guards.

HALLOWEEN

What's causing noises
in the kitchen? --kittens or
Halloween goblins?

SWALLOWS

Two swallows fly in
to get out of the weather;
one cat -- two swallows.

CATATINATIONS*

Catatinations:
unceremoniously
hauled away and dumped!

*Catatination: a sackful of rowdy and contentious cats with a
penchant for midnight madness.

Harry the Cat I

Several swallows
swoop down to harry the cat.
Why harry Harry?

HARRY THE CAT II

Why harry Harry?
He's just doing what cats do:
he swallows swallows!

BEES

Bee or not to Bee?
That is the question. . . for cats
who've ever been stung.

SUN SPOTS

Basking in the sun's
hard work for cats preferring
to lie in the shade.

Inheritance

Sick, scrawny, hungry,
flea bitten, worm infested--
he shares the Pure Gold.

KITTY JOY

Where opposites meet--
consummate joy and carnage!
Torn butterfly wings . . .

TURKEY TIME

Thanksgiving table
loaded with festive delight . . .
Cats, stay out of sight!

FLOODS

Warm rains and snow-melt
loose the grip of mid-winter,
so here come the floods!

EVERY YEAR

River's a-risin'!
Kittens livin' in flood plains
gonna get wet feet!

SPIRIT OF HAIKU

Spirit of Haiku
likes to make himself at home:
my unbidden muse.

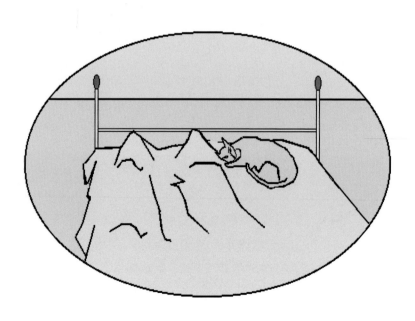

FLIGHT

Spirit and Shadow
slip into the forest night;
rustling wings take flight.

LOVE

Kitty Karlyle shrieks
and sings to the stars above.
Ol' Roger's in love.

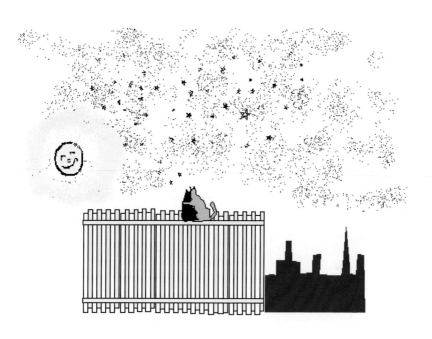

QUESTION

In any language—
La nuit tous les chats sont gris.
--so what's there to see?

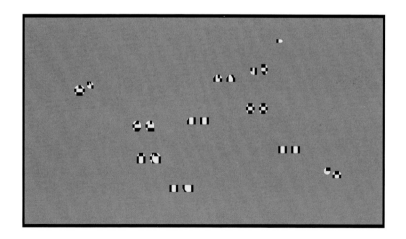

PUMPKIN TIME

Time for Hallowe'en:
witches' black cats can be seen
"Mephistopheling!"

CANTALOUPES

Cats and cantaloupes:
now there's a combination!
Melons are mellow . . .

Mystery solved?

Teleportation:
the obvious solution
to many puzzles.

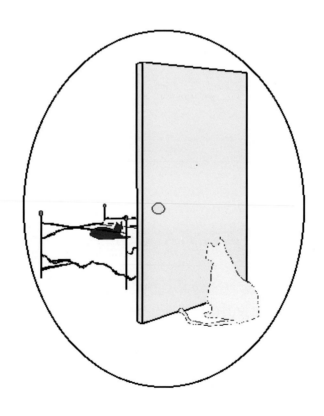

TRIBUTE

Here's to Ol' Riley—
not for the fact he's dead, but
for the life he led.

DILEMMA?

More is less and less
is more?   Then beggars are rich
and Fat Cats are poor!

A SERIOUS TRUTH

Serendipity:
is no ordinary thing;
it's the "cat's mee-ow!"